CY

NANO

CY Nano Handbook
Copyright © 2010 Christianity Explored

www.christianityexplored.org

CHRISTIANITY EXPLORED

Published by:
The Good Book Company Ltd
Elm House, 37 Elm Road, New Malden, Surrey KT3 3HB, UK
Tel: 0845 225 0880; International: +44 (0) 208 942 0880
email: admin@thegoodbook.co.uk

Websites:
UK: www.thegoodbook.co.uk
N America: www.thegoodbook.com
Australia: www.thegoodbook.com.au
New Zealand: www.thegoodbook.co.nz

Unless otherwise indicated, Scripture is taken from
the HOLY BIBLE, NEW INTERNATIONAL VERSION
Copyright © 1973, 1978, 1984 International Bible Society
Used by permission of Zondervan Bible Publishers

All rights reserved. Except as may be permitted by the Copyright Act, no portion of this publication may be reproduced in any form or by any means without prior permission from the publisher
ISBN: 9781907377150

Design by Steve Devane and André Parker
Illustrations by Alex Webb-Peploe

Printed in the UK

HANDBOOK

explore

1

CY it's worth exploring

If you could ask God one question, and you knew it would be answered, what would it be?

❯ CY it's worth exploring   CY Jesus matters   CY Jesus came   CY Jesus died

READ MARK 1:1

What does Mark say Christianity is all about in the first sentence of his book?

How is that different from some of the pictures we've drawn?

download

- Christianity is not about rules or ceremonies. It's all about Jesus Christ.
- If we're here by chance, we don't matter or have any value. But God created us – so we matter enormously.
- We all face death sooner or later. Since we all have to die, what's the point of living?
- The Bible says we don't really start living until we know the one who made us, and live as he made us to live.
- But how can we get to know God? We need him to show himself to us. Mark says he's done that for us by sending Jesus Christ. If we want to know what God's like, we must look at Jesus.
- That's why "the gospel about Jesus Christ" is good news.

> CY it's worth exploring   CY Jesus matters   CY Jesus came   CY Jesus died

talkback

If you asked a group of people in the street: "What's the point of life?", what kind of answers would you get?

What do most people think about God and Christianity?
✔ your answers
Why do you think that is?

- boring
- pointless
- out of date
- full of rules
- important
- only for Sundays
- interesting
- same as other religions
- your own suggestion here

What about Jesus? Do people think he matters? What do *you* think?

Do you want the good news or the bad news first?

Ugh... bad news, I guess.

The bad news is... there's no good news!! Ha Ha!!

Well, that's 30 seconds of my life I'll never get back.

CY Jesus lives   CY God accepts us   Inside track   CY We should believe

7

2 CY Jesus matters

explore

Think of your best friend. What do you really like about them?

READ MARK 2:1–12

Why is the house full at the start of this story?
(Look at Mark 1:45 for clues.)

Imagine you're in the room. How would you have felt when Jesus said: "Son, your sins are forgiven"? (See verse 5.) Why do you think he said it?

Why do the religious leaders get so upset when Jesus forgives the man's sin? (See verse 7.) Do you think they are right?

Jesus heals the man so that he can walk. What's the real reason Jesus healed him? (Look at verse 10 for a clue.)

download

- Mark 1:1 says that Jesus is the "Christ" – which means the chosen one of God, God's promised King – and "the Son of God". Mark then shows us that:
- Jesus can forgive sins – Mark 2:1–10
- Jesus has power to heal – Mark 2:11–12
- Jesus has power over nature – Mark 4:35–41
- Jesus has power over demons – Mark 5:1–17
- Jesus has power over death – Mark 5:35–42

CY it's worth exploring   ● CY Jesus matters   CY Jesus came   CY Jesus died

Which of the events Mark tells us about would you have found most amazing or scary? Why?

What do *you* think of Jesus?

talkback

QUIET! BE STILL!

No, it's definitely not working.

explore

3 CY Jesus came

What do you think is the biggest problem facing the world?

From last time's *CY Nano*, what does Jesus think is the biggest problem facing the world?

READ MARK 12:28–31

What does it mean to love God with all your heart, with all your soul, with all your mind and with all your strength?

What does it mean to love your neighbour as yourself?

How good do you think you are at living up to these two commands? Where do you especially mess up?

download

- Jesus came to deal with our biggest problem: our sin (Mark 2:17).
- Each and every one of us rebels against our loving Creator. That rebellion is what the Bible calls "sin".
- Sin is a serious problem that will lead us to hell. If we continue to reject God, then he will respond to that decision – and reject us.
- Only Jesus can rescue us from the problem of sin. Jesus came to rescue rebels.

CY it's worth exploring CY Jesus matters ❱ **CY Jesus came** CY Jesus died

talkback

Do you think sin is a problem? Why or why not?

How would you feel if all your thoughts, words and actions were on display for everyone to see?

4

CY Jesus died

Imagine you know how and when you will die. How would it make you feel? What would it make you do?

READ MARK 8:27–33

What does Peter realize in verse 29?

Why would Jesus' words in verse 31 surprise Peter?

Why does Jesus confront Peter in verse 33?

When Jesus died on the cross, was it unexpected?
(Look at Mark 9:31 and Mark 10:33–34 for clues.)

download

- Jesus knew when he was going to die. His death wasn't an accident – it was planned.
- Jesus' death is the only way we can be saved from our sin. It is the way Jesus rescues us, as "a ransom for many" (Mark 10:45).
- When Jesus died, he was willingly taking the punishment for *our* sin. He was punished in *our* place, so that *we* can be rescued.
- Jesus' death makes it possible for us to be accepted by God and enjoy a friendship with him.
- People have different reactions to Jesus' death: Pontius Pilate goes with the crowd; the soldiers are wrapped up in themselves; the religious leaders think they don't need Jesus; the Roman centurion gets it right, when he says that Jesus is "the Son of God".

How would you feel if someone else deliberately took the punishment for something serious you had done wrong?

Why do you think Jesus' death on the cross is so important to Christians?

Which of the reactions to Jesus' death is most like your reaction?

talkback

explore

5 CY Jesus lives

What would be your first reaction if you heard someone had come back from the dead?

READ MARK 15:42 – 16:8

Why are the women worried as they approach the tomb? (See Mark 16:3.)

CY it's worth exploring   CY Jesus matters   CY Jesus came   CY Jesus died

Find four things that surprise them when they arrive. (See verses 4–6.)

Should they have been surprised that Jesus rose from the dead?
(Look at Mark 8:31, 9:30–31, 10:32–34 for clues.)

Why do you think the women ran away from the tomb?

download

- If Jesus has not risen from the dead, Christianity collapses.
- The resurrection proves that Jesus is who he says he is, and that his death was a ransom for many.
- Jesus did die: Pontius Pilate, the Roman centurion, Joseph of Arimathea and the women were all certain that Jesus had died.
- Jesus did rise: the tomb was empty; Jesus was seen alive by hundreds of people, many of whom were later killed for insisting that he was alive.
- The resurrection proves that Jesus will come again as Judge of the whole world (Acts 17:31).
- The resurrection means that death has been defeated. If we trust in Jesus, we can be sure that God will raise us from death.

CY it's worth exploring   CY Jesus matters   CY Jesus came   CY Jesus died

What part of the evidence for Jesus' resurrection do you find most convincing? Why?

Do you think that Jesus rose from the dead? Why or why not?

Why does Jesus' resurrection matter, if at all?

talkback

> CY Jesus lives   CY God accepts us   Inside track   CY We should believe

explore

6 CY God accepts us

What things do people do so others will accept them?

What things do people do to be accepted by God?

READ MARK 10:17–22

Why does the man think God should accept him?

What is Jesus' response?

Why does the man leave? What does that show about the man?

download

If God asked you: "Why should I give you eternal life?", what would you say?

- Most people think God will accept them because of things they have done or haven't done. But these things can't solve the problem of sin.
- The Bible tells us that God accepts us, not because of anything *we've* done, but because of what *Jesus* has done.
- Like the man with the skin disease, we need to ask Jesus to make us clean (Mark 1:40-42).
- The only way we can be accepted by God is because he sent Jesus to die on the cross in our place.
- Grace is God's undeserved gift to us. Because of what Jesus has done, God treats us in a way we don't deserve.

talkback

What exactly is grace? How would you explain it if someone asked you?

What do people find offensive about grace? What does it say about us?

What is so great about grace? What does it offer us?

What does grace tell us about what God is like?

CY Jesus lives ▸ CY God accepts us   Inside track   CY we should believe

CY you need the Holy Spirit

- The Holy Spirit, who comes to live in Christians, is the Spirit of Jesus himself – the Holy Spirit is God.
- The Holy Spirit helps us in a number of ways including:
  - guiding followers of Jesus
  - showing people their sin
  - changing people so they want to please God.
- Jesus promises that when we trust in him, he will come and live in us forever by his Spirit (John 14:15-17).

talkback

Before *CY Nano*, what did you know about the Holy Spirit?

What did you find most surprising about who the Holy Spirit is or what the Holy Spirit does?

How do you feel about the Spirit of Jesus coming to live "with you" and "in you"? (John 14:17)

● Inside track

CY the church is your family

- In the Bible, "the church" is not a building – it's a group of Christians who follow Christ together.
- The Holy Spirit unites Christians as members of God's family.
- If we're to live the Christian life, we need to help each other.
- A good church is where Christians listen carefully to God's word – the Bible – and change how they think and live as a result. They also encourage each other, remember Jesus' death and resurrection, and pray together.

CY it's worth exploring   CY Jesus matters   CY Jesus came   CY Jesus died

talkback

What has church been like for you? Has your experience of church been good or not so good?

What do you think God's *should* family be like?

How do you think a good church will help someone who's trying to follow Jesus?

> Inside track

CY it's good to talk

- The Bible and prayer are really important for Christians. When we read the Bible, God talks to us. When we pray, we talk to God.
- The Bible helps us to be strong and to keep going in the Christian life.
- Christians can pray to God about anything, knowing that he is in control of everything.

talkback

Have you read any parts of the Bible? What did you like about them? What did you find difficult?

Do you ever pray? What kind of things do you say to God? When are you most likely to talk to God?

What do you think you might find most difficult about praying and reading the Bible?

CY Jesus lives   CY God accepts us   ❯ Inside track   CY we should believe *explore*

7

CY we should believe

We started *CY Nano* by asking: "If you could ask God one question, what would it be?"
If God were to ask you one question, what do you think it would be?

READ MARK 1:14–15

What do you think Jesus means by "the good news of God"?

What does Jesus mean when he says: "The time has come" and "The kingdom of God is near"?

What do you think the word "repent" means?

What do you think it means to "believe the good news"?

download

- A Christian is someone who knows who Jesus is: the Son of God, the "Christ", the King who was promised throughout the Old Testament.

- A Christian is someone who understands why Jesus came: he came to die as the only way sinful people can be brought back into a friendship with God.

- A Christian is someone who follows Jesus: Jesus says: "If anyone would come after me, he must deny himself and take up his cross and follow me" (Mark 8:34). Denying self means no longer living for ourselves but for Jesus and others. Taking up our cross means being prepared to follow him, whatever the cost.

- Jesus gives a convincing reason to live like this: "Whoever loses his life for me and for the gospel will save it" (Mark 8:35). If we give our lives to him, he will save them. We will know and enjoy God now, and spend eternity with him when we die.

How would you score the following statements?
(0 = completely unconvinced, 10 = very sure)

Jesus is God.

Jesus came to rescue us from our sin.

Following Jesus means denying ourselves and putting Jesus first, whatever the cost.

What choices will you make now that you've finished CY Nano? What are you going to do next?

talkback

CY Jesus lives   CY God accepts us   Inside track   ● CY we should believe   37

explore

The Mark challenge

You can read through Mark's Gospel in less than two hours. But to really think about what he is telling us about Jesus, it is better to take it slowly. Use the reading plan below to work your way through Mark, taking time to think about what you read.

- ☐ **Day 1.** Mark 1:1-28
- ☐ **Day 2.** Mark 1:29 – 2:12
- ☐ **Day 3.** Mark 2:13 – 3:6
- ☐ **Day 4.** Mark 3:7-35
- ☐ **Day 5.** Mark 4:1-41
- ☐ **Day 6.** Mark 5:1-20
- ☐ **Day 7.** Mark 5:21-43
- ☐ **Day 8.** Mark 6:1-29
- ☐ **Day 9.** Mark 6:30-56
- ☐ **Day 10.** Mark 7:1-37
- ☐ **Day 11.** Mark 8:1-38
- ☐ **Day 12.** Mark 9:1-32
- ☐ **Day 13.** Mark 9:33 – 10:16
- ☐ **Day 14.** Mark 10:17-52
- ☐ **Day 15.** Mark 11:1-33
- ☐ **Day 16.** Mark 12:1-44
- ☐ **Day 17.** Mark 13:1-37
- ☐ **Day 18.** Mark 14:1-52
- ☐ **Day 19.** Mark 14:53 – 15:15
- ☐ **Day 20.** Mark 15:16-47
- ☐ **Day 21.** Mark 16

A note about chapters and verses

Throughout Mark's book you will see some large numbers and some smaller numbers. The larger numbers are the chapters Mark has been split into. The smaller numbers are the verses that make up each chapter. The chapters and verses weren't in the original but have been added later to help us find our way around. We often use a kind of shorthand so that Mark chapter 1 and verse 1 will be written as **"Mark 1:1"** or sometimes as **"Mark 1 v 1"**.

map it out

Mark tells us about the amazing things Jesus did and said. He also tells us where Jesus was at the time. Use the map to help you follow the story as Jesus travels around the country of Israel.

Notes:

The Great Sea (Mediterranean Sea)

- Sidon
- Tyre
- Caesarea Philippi

GALILEE
- Capernaum
- Bethsaida
- Nazareth

Gadara

Decapolis

SAMARIA

- Jericho
- **Jerusalem**
- Bethlehem
- Bethany

JUDEA

0 10 20 30 50 km